BINKY'S TROPHY

THE STORY OF AN ALASKAN POLAR BEAR

Written and Illustrated

by

Millie Spezialy

Six Suns Publishing Company
Anchorage

To

**My husband, Dom, and my sister Eilleen,
two special cheerleaders in my life**

and

**Dick, Barb, Bonnie, and Nanette,
for their encouraging words**

and to

Binky

Published by Six Suns Publishing Co.
P.O. Box 112852
Anchorage, Alaska 99511-2852
Library discounts available

Publisher Cataloging-in-Publication Data
Spezialy, Millie.
Binky's Trophy, The Story of an Alaskan Polar Bear
written and illustrated by Millie Spezialy—1st ed.
[32]p: col. ill.: cm.

Summary: An orphaned Alaskan polar bear cub adjusts
to his new environment while keeping a family tradition alive.
1. Alaskan polar bear cub. Arctic environment. Juvenile fiction.
2. Alaskan polar bear cub adjusting to a new environment. Juvenile fiction.
3. Alaskan polar bear-family genealogy. Juvenile fiction.

Library of Congress Catalog Card Number 96-92525

ISBN -0-9654200-1-9

Book designed by Jim Tilly, Art & International Productions, LLC, Anchorage.
Art direction by Nanette Stevenson.
Illustrations in watercolor.

First Edition 1996
10 9 8 7 6 5 4 3 2 1

PRINTED IN
HONG KONG

Photo by Stacy Lackie

Binky, a polar bear cub, was orphaned near the Beaufort Sea in 1974 and brought to the Alaska Zoo in Anchorage.

The Alaska Zoo, incorporated in 1968 to care for injured or orphaned animals, welcomed the little polar bear into the zoo family. The Anchorage community rallied together to build Binky a new habitat at the zoo.

Binky was an exceptional bear. His majestic spirit, proud and strong, captivated all who came to see him. He was loved by children and grown-ups alike.

Binky became a folk hero after his encounter with a tourist from Australia. Newspapers as far away as Hong Kong carried the story and picture of Binky holding the tourist's shoe. People rallied to his defense from all over the world, saying, "Don't let them hurt Binky because of someone's mistake."

In July of 1995 Binky and his companion, Nuka, fell ill. The entire zoo community fought to save them, but to no avail.

The grief that was felt when Binky died was incredible. Children brought flowers and pictures and they cried. Adults were also very emotional. On the day of his memorial service, thousands stood in the rain around Binky's home to listen to the eulogy given by Bill Tobin, longtime Alaskan and former *Anchorage Times* editor.

We all loved Binky dearly. We miss him.

Sammye Seawell

Sammye Seawell
Director of the Alaska Zoo
Anchorage, June, 1996

Binky's head turned left and right, left and right,
as he searched the Arctic darkness.
   "Mother-r-r-r," he cried.
   Only the silent north wind heard his call.

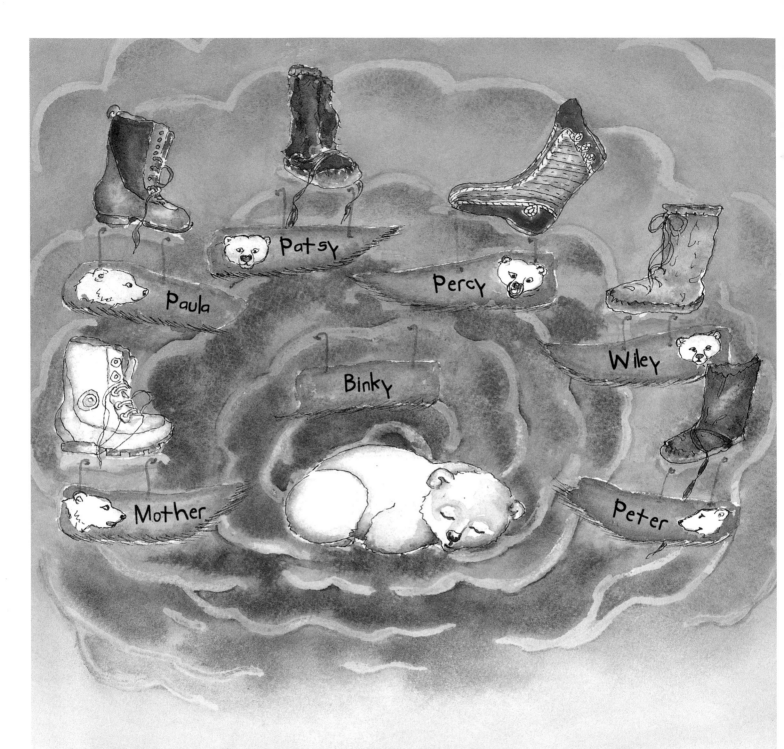

Shivering, Binky backed into his den and curled up beneath the trophy wall. Seeing the familiar boots comforted him. Unlike most polar bears, his family collected boots. Every night he would ask his mother, "Tell me again how each of the boots was collected."

"Practice and patience," she'd say. "That's what it takes to get a good trophy."

Tonight there would be no story. Mother was missing.

The next morning, Binky was still asleep when someone called
down into the den.

"Hey, Binky, the sun's up," called his friend, Artie, the Arctic fox.

"Has your mother returned yet?"

"No. She's been gone a long time. I miss her so much."

"Come on, I'll help you catch breakfast," Artie yelled,
bounding after a snowshoe hare.

"Here I come," cried Binky, joining the chase.

"Got you!" Binky roared and dove for the hare.
SWOOSH, down the slippery hill he went.
Binky's breakfast quickly disappeared.
"Next time," Artie said patiently.
"Yes," thought Binky, "next time I'll do better."

What else could he eat?

"Gawk, ka-blunk, ka-blunk," came a raven's call.

"This time I've got you," Binky whispered without moving.

"Gawk, ka-blunk, ka-blunk." The raven flew closer.

Binky pounced.

"Gawk, gawk, gawk," rasped the raven as he wiggled free, leaving only a coal-black feather behind.

A hungry little bear returned to his den that night. Binky
pulled the whaler's boot down from the trophy wall and
savored the last drops of oil he found on the bottom.
"Mother will come soon," he growled softly to himself.

Next morning, Binky awoke to a loud roar. "Mother's home," he yelped, happily tumbling from the den to greet her. He never heard Snappy Owl's warning hoot. Or felt the tranquilizing dart.

"Looks like you haven't eaten for a while," sighed the wildlife manager, picking up the tiny cub. "Poor little orphan. I know a place where you'll be safe."

Binky awoke confused. Where was he? He felt strange paws holding him. He tried to wiggle free.

"Hey, little fellow, easy. You're safe here," said the gentle stranger.

"My name is Jim. I bet you're hungry."

Tasting the warm milk, Binky grabbed for the bottle, but his wild swing sent it flying.

"Hold on, little guy. With a little practice and patience, you'll get it right." Binky grabbed hungrily. This time the top came loose. SWOOSH. The milk poured over his face. Binky was surprised.

"Let's try again," said Jim as he picked up another bottle.

"The raccoon's cage will be your home until we can build you
a better one," said Jim.

Binky looked around the small cage and wailed. "This can't be home."

No mother. No trophy wall. Where is the pack ice?

Where is the cold, blue water?

In the two years it took to build his den, Binky grew to adolescence.
Finally his new home and pool were ready. Moving day had arrived.
Seeing open water, Binky dove in and swam around.
  "Aah!" he roared happily.

After his refreshing swim, Binky napped by the pool. Memories of home
filled his mind. He dreamt that he was with his mother on the Beaufort pack ice.
"Tell me how each of the boots was collected," he pleaded.
His mother's voice filled his dreams as she retold his favorite family story.

"Long ago, Alaska was warm. Peter Polar Bear saw a new creature near the marsh. What was it? It had something on its paws. Peter was curious and followed it.

'Oh, no, a beast!' shrieked the the frightened creature.

With a rumbling growl, powerful Peter pounced and turned the creature upside down. He tugged off one of the things on its paws and carried it home.

The creature's buckskin boot wouldn't fit over Peter's sharp claws. He hung it on the wall. It became the first trophy.

After that each generation of bears took pride in adding a new boot to the collection.

Alaska's climate changed. The weather became colder and colder. Eskimos came looking for food. Patsy Polar Bear crept across the ice for hours before she snatched her prize.

Stalking a seal, the Eskimo hunter never looked behind him until it was too late.

SLIP, SLIDE. And his furry boot was gone!

Many years passed before new people came in search of fur seals. Percy Polar Bear watched the Russian ship glide among the ice floes.

'A good place to hunt,' said the sailor as he stepped from the ship.

He was startled when the ice turned into a fierce, white whirlwind with long claws.

'Set sail before the storm overtakes us!' he shouted through trembling lips as he leaped up the ladder and onto the deck.

A red-and-black, felt boot joined the family collection.

"More years passed," Mother said. "Next, hunters came looking for whales." She took down an old whaler's boot.

"Maybe you can find a little oil on the bottom of this boot," she said with a sly grin. Binky never suspected that his mother rubbed fresh oil over the boot whenever she could. The oil was like candy to him.

Mother continued. "The scent of fresh whale blubber led Wiley Polar Bear to the whaling ship. He lay motionless on the white ice, his paw covering his black nose.

SNIP, SNAP! Wiley pulled the slick, waterproof boot off the startled man.

'The ice is alive,' screamed the captain, who shivered and shook in fright."

Mother plucked the wrinkled leather boot from the wall.
CLINK, CLUNK, CLINK went the shiny nuggets deep
inside the toe. Binky heard the familiar sounds of his first rattle.
"Paula Polar Bear found this treasure while walking on
the beach at Nome. She saw a man washing pebbles in a pan.
'Eureka, it's gold,' sang he, 'and it's all for me.'
SWISH, SWASH. She spun the miner around
and pulled off his muddy leather boot. Paula was seen
loping down the beach, her trophy held high."

"Of course," mother chuckled, "getting my trophy during an Arctic storm wasn't easy.

New travelers in our land stood still and looked into the sky for enemy planes. Their white clothing made it almost impossible to see them. I was hunting near the shore when I got caught in a blizzard. Dropping to my belly, I saw this BIG WHITE BOOT in front of my nose. With a quick pounce, I plucked this prize.

'It was a monster, white and fierce,' cried the guardsman, to all who would listen."

The sound of voices woke Binky from his long dream. He peered through the bars. He saw a crowd of people with boots of every shape and size.

"My trophy," he yelled and rushed toward them. Hitting the bars with a crunch, he fell back in surprise.

Wide awake now, and remembering where he was, Binky retreated to the back of the cage. He had let the family down. "I'll never get my trophy," he groaned sadly.

The years passed and Binky turned into a giant like his father. He loved winters best. It was cold and dark.

People came from all over the world to see him. "He's lord of the Arctic," they'd say as they watched Binky walk like a king around his enclosure.

Soon he was famous. Binky took it in stride. Being a celebrity didn't change him at all.

Summertime brought noise, heat, and crowds.
"What a handsome bear," the people said.
"So big."
"Look at those huge paws."
"Grrrr...rrrr," Binky roared.
His picture was in the newspaper and on television.
Everyone loved Binky.

Then, one summer day…
"What a beautiful bear," he heard a voice say.

Ignoring the warning signs, the woman climbed over the wooden fence.
Binky's eyes widened ever so slightly.

"Now I can get a better picture," said the visitor,
putting her camera between the bars of the cage.
    Suddenly, all fifteen hundred pounds of powerful polar bear
were in motion. Binky was swift and sure.

In a split second, he had his prize.

"What was that?" screamed the startled woman as she was pulled away from the cage.

Binky, head held high, strutted around clutching his trophy for all to see. The family tradition was alive and well.

Binky was a proud polar bear that day.